Peter Tully's

PICTURES of PAIGNTON

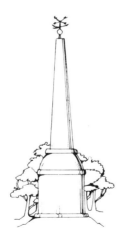

OBELISK PUBLICATIONS

I should like to dedicate this book to the memory of Mr Henry Slater who was my mentor and great photographic friend.

Other Obelisk Publications

Around & About the Haldon Hills, Chips Barber
The Lost City of Exeter, Chips Barber
Diary of a Dartmoor Walker, Chips Barber
Adventure Through Red Devon, Raymond B Cattell
An Exeter Boyhood, Frank Retter
The Torbay Book, Chips Barber
Under Sail through South Devon & Dartmoor, R. B. Cattell
The Great Walks of Dartmoor, Terry Bound
Ide, Bill Rowland
Diary of a Devonshire Walker, Chips Barber
Rambling in the Plymouth Countryside, Lister & Woolley
The Great Little Dartmoor Book, Chips Barber
Tales of the Unexplained in Devon, Judy Chard
The Great Little Exeter Book, Chips Barber
The DevonAir Book of Family Walks, Chips Barber
Running in Devon, John Legge
Memories of Newton Abbot, Elsie Townsend
Albert Labbett's Crediton Collection
DevonAir Book of Haunted Happenings, Judy Chard
Made in Devon, Chips Barber & David FitzGerald

Dartmoor in Colour, Chips Barber
Burgh Island & Bigbury Bay, Chips Barber & Judy Chard
Dark and Dastardly Dartmoor, Sally and Chips Barber
Talking about Topsham, Sara Vernon
An Alphington Album, Pauline Aplin & Jeanne Gaskell

First Published in 1988 by Obelisk Publications,
2 Church Hill, Pinhoe, Exeter, Devon
Printed in Great Britain by Penwell Ltd, Parkwood, Callington, Cornwall.
©Peter Tully 1988

The oldest part of Paignton is in the area around Church Street, Winner Street and here at Well Street. This is a fine picture taken about the turn of the century. With the flags hanging from the windows of the houses, it is obvious that some Royal or patriotic occasion is being celebrated.

Winner Street is a short distance away and this photograph of it was probably taken about 1880 and shows the Rocklight Paraffin wagon, a familiar sight to Paignton's Victorian residents, outside Dellers Stores. In this picture Osborn's store occupies the corner site which became the Co-op Society many years later.

Known to most people who remember it as Miss Evans' Drapery Shop, this building once stood at the top of Church Street at its junction with Winner Street. It was demolished in the 1960s and had shops on three sides.

This is Palace Avenue taken about 1900. There were private houses on all sides along with the newly built Methodist Church and the Public Hall surrounding the charming gardens. It is interesting to compare the size of the monkey puzzle tree with its height today. The original houses were eventually converted into shops.

Bought, designed and built by a consortium of Bridgman, Lambshead and Couldrey, such developments by local entrepreneurs were common.

This is Paignton's second police station (not counting the "Clink" in Littlegate Road which served as a parish prison for local delinquents). The first police station was attached to the Old Town Hall in Totnes Road, built in 1870. This one was built at the turn of the century in Palace Avenue and was demolished in the early 1970s, to be replaced by Westminster House, the present police station being in Blatchcombe Road.

Here we have two views of Palace Avenue pictured ninety years apart. This photograph is taken during the winter blizzard of 1898. Very little change has taken place apart from bowing to the inevitable march of motor transport.

This wintry scene from 1978 is fortunately an unusual sight for this part of England.

This is the South side of Palace Avenue looking towards the old post office. It shows the Cash Tailoring Co. which became Thorn's, next door to the gas company and now the home of the Trustee Savings Bank and Barclay's Bank. Church's China Shop is still there. The original plan was to build the Public Hall in the middle of the Gardens, but this was abandoned in favour of its present site at the head of the Avenue. The PUDC acquired the Public Hall from its private owners in 1920.

"The Progress" was Paignton's first steam bus with Tom Adams its driver. This photo was taken in the early 1900s outside Moores' Hotel, which later became Browns, and is now the Coverdale Hotel in Dartmouth Road.

This photograph is taken in Victoria Square in about 1880. The Gerstons, shown here with the Naval Bank on the corner, were constructed at the junction of the Torquay, Totnes and Dartmouth turnpikes, hence the names the roads still bear today. The developers who built Prestos in Victoria Park wanted to name their precinct Victoria Square but were quietly reminded that we already had one. In truth it is more commonly known amongst old Paigntonians as Maypole Corner.

The reason why it is called Maypole Corner is that in the days when Paignton boasted a Home and Colonial, a Liptons and International Stores, Maypole Dairy Ltd, took over the premises of the Naval Bank but later moved down into Victoria Street.

The view from Winner Hill overlooking Winner Street in the foreground shows Palace Avenue as a field! The house on the right beyond the field was turned into his butcher's shop by Mr Foale in 1887 and is now Tescos. The big tree on the left of it stands in what is now Victoria Street, but was then known as Station Road, one of the two roads made up by the Railway Company, the other being Town Bank (now Torbay Road).

Queen's Park was another undeveloped area, a wasteland of marsh and ozier beds. This view looks towards Torbay Road during the early 1900s. "Streaky Bacon Terrace" was so named because of its lines of red and white bricks, and has since had most of its ground floors turned into shops. Town Bark Terrace lies further towards the front, and the south side of Torbay Road is shown creeping up towards the railway. Garfield Road divides the two terraces.

Hyde Dendy's Gerston Hotel was built in 1870 and had still to be extended further towards the Railway. On the right the Broadmead Hotel had yet to be demolished to make room for the Picture House. Garfield Terrace had been designed and built by Bridgman whilst Victoria Street was still a grassy field. The leisurely scene is a far cry from today.

The troops shown leaving Paignton Station for France during World War I were possibly the First Field Ambulance Division. Note the newly built Paignton Picture House, the first purpose built cinema in the West Country.

Nell Pope's Railway Temperance Hotel and Cafe in Torbay Road is pictured here in the 1890s. The iron railway footbridge (replacing the original wood one) remained until the 1970s. The Gerston Hotel extended towards the railway on the site now occupied by Woolworth.

Station Square in the "P aring 20s" looks to be almost as busy and congested with traffic as it is today! Horse drawn hackney carriages mixed with the motor vehicles. Neil Pope's has become May's Bakery and Cafe, more recently renamed the "Off the Rails" restaurant.

F W Woolworth arrived on the scene in Paignton in the early 1930s. Their first store in Station Square, as shown in the picture, was demolished in 1964 to make way for the present building.

Street parking in the 1930s was no problem for patrons of Dellers Cafe, Torbay Road. Built by Lambshead in 1911, this magnificent building was sadly demolished in 1965 to be replaced by a very lack-lustre block of shops with flats above. Fortunately Queens Park Mansions, situated between the site of Dellers and the present Torbay Cinema, remains as a visible tribute to the Lambshead family to whom Paignton owed much of its prosperity.

Stentifords Corner is now impersonally known as Hyde Road Corner. With the end of the trams in 1934, the shop shown was knocked down and reconstructed about 15 feet to the right. There were no shops on the left hand side of Torquay Road.

Traffic passing along Torquay road between Victoria Street and Hyde Road in the 1960s was two-way. The no waiting sign indicated alternate days for parking on the side—a metal flap was changed each morning. On the right of the picture is Newstead House which was an auxiliary hospital for many wounded servicemen during World War I, manned by nursing volunteers. It was later occupied by Mr Griffin the dentist, then by Mr Bain. It was demolished at the same time as Croft Terrace to make way for Crossways Shopping Centre and the new Post Office in 1963. Mr Martin's furniture shop on the right is now the Halifax Building Society.

44082. PAIGNTON: OLD COTTAGES.

These cottages in Southfield Road at the junction of Shorton Road were pulled down in the 1950s to widen the route towards Polsham Road.

Preston, near Paignton

77662,

This old postcard view of Torquay Road, Preston was taken from the junction of Seaway Road. Now shops, the houses on the right led up to the Tram Depot, which now houses Skippers & Glover's Tyre Depot. Traffic lights were installed here in the early 1930s. Lloyds Bank, Preston Branch, was built at these crossroads, the architect was the grandson of G.S. Bridgman.

Preston near Paignton

This is a different view of Seaway Road taken about 1910. In the open space several roads now link with it. Morin and Eugene Roads come in from the left and Orient Road emerges from the right. At the top of Seaway Road with its junction with Torquay Road stood the old turnpike toll house, later to become a branch of the ubiquitous Chards Bros Stores.

Perhaps not all changes are for the worse! This industrial scene photographed in 1936 shows the Torquay and Paignton Gas Light and Coke Company's Hollacombe Works. The retort house and gas holders have now gone, to be replaced by landscaped gardens.

In 1877 Paris Singer agreed to build a retaining wall of huge limestone blocks along Preston Sea Front. Messrs. Yeos of Plymouth were the main contractors, with Mr Yeo himself supervising the work (centre on wall, arms akimbo). Note the artisans with their bowler hats, whilst the workmen sported soft hats or caps. Over 100 years later the sea wall requires minimal maintenance.

A frequent visitor to the town was Hancock's Fair seen here on Paignton North Green about 1900. Beyond the fairground Villa Marina had yet to be built in the grounds of Redcliffe Towers. Note the Showman's tractor built into the set of Hancock's Living Picture Palace. A horse grazes behind the small living vans. Anderton & Rowlands Fair replaced Hancocks in the 1920s following a disastrous fire in Plymouth which destroyed the latter's equipment.

Hyde Dendy was a very active man in Paignton life. Here is his Esplanade Hotel with a sign on the right above the entrance to the Torbay Cycling track built 1883. It was laid out behind the hotel and much used for national competitions. Formerly two villas, Dendy joined them with his main entrance, surmounted it with a tower, and added the "dormitory block" on the left, I suspect using similar plans drawn up for the Gerston Hotel. It became the Prince Regent, now The Inn on the Green.

This revealing and panoramic view is from Primley Park looking NE across Tor Bay. The grandstand of the Cycle Track behind the Esplanade Hotel can be seen in the middle distance. The square roof in the middle of the picture is the Public Hall, now Palace Avenue Theatre. The buildings behind the foreground shrubbery are in Winner Street and the row of villas to the right of Church Tower are in Polsham Park.

This is Paignton Sea Front about 1902 showing the Regatta Fair on Central Green. Mrs Penwill, to the left of the picture, paid ten shillings per season to set up her drinks stall on the sands. The first shelters erected in 1892 cost just under £100 each.

Paignton Pier fire started at noon one day and was still burning the next day! With considerable money to invest in Paignton earned in the industrial Midlands, Hyde Dendy built his promenade pier in 1878. It complemented his bathing machines and steamer to Torquay. However, at about mid-day on Thursday 18 June 1919 smoke was seen coming from the pavilion on the seaward end of the pier, and before the brass helmeted firemen could reach the scene with their horse drawn Shard Mason fire engine, the grand piano and most of the structure had plummeted into the sea.

This is one of the few photographs of Torbay House, built about 1805 on the site of an old Ale House. We believe that so many seamen, who had come ashore from vessels anchored in Tor Bay to sample the local cider, met an untimely end in the marshes or were dealt an unfriendly blow by the local inhabitants, that an ale house was built on the foreshore for their use. There seems to be no other explanation for a pub to be set so far from town, years before Town Bank had been thought of. Torbay House was purchased by Mr Fletcher, another Birmingham solicitor like Hyde Dendy in 1865, and demolished by him in 1877. The stone recovered was used to build Adelphi Terrace. This picture, probably dated 1860, shows the wide expanse of fields which backed the town at that time.

Paignton Harbour &c.

The Preventative House at Paignton was the home of the local customs and excise men in the late 1800s, and is now used as a toilet block—complete with original doors. Many a barrel of brandy came ashore along the coast, particularly at Goodrington, where the level beaches made it easy for a small boat to unload a dozen or so barrels of French cognac, to be stowed away in a cart or barrow, finally to be brought to light in a local hostelry or fisherman's cottage on a dark and stormy night. The Harbour at Paignton received its first vessel in 1839 with imports of coal, wood and stone, and exports of cider, cabbages and some fish. Purchased from the Paignton Harbour Co in 1936, the PUDC appointed Miss Stella Gale to be Harbour Master—the only woman to hold such a post in the British Isles, and at that time (with no equality of opportunity) this was no mean feat!

These cottages at the south end of Paignton Sea Front were demolished in 1882 to build the Paignton Club. The raised, open land beyond the cottages is now Cleveland Road.

This is one of the best photographs of Cliff Cottage and was taken in 1890. Numerous painters have tried to portray the thatch on the outhouse but have failed. The camera was unsuccessful too! The cottage exists today, although on top of a high bank. The path that led up to the front door was removed, along with several hundred tons of soil, to enable the road surrounding the harbour to join up with Marsh Lane, now Sands Road.

Torbay Road, Paignton.

Torbay Road was a quiet thoroughfare in 1912 when this postcard view was taken. There is a canopy over the shops on the northern side of the road, and the south side pavement is very wide. Deller's Cafe had been completed by this date and can be seen just to the right of the centre.

This is an earlier picture of Torbay Road taken about 1903. The drinking fountain and lamp, commemorating Queen Victoria's Golden Jubilee of 1887, was lost during the building of the Festival Hall. Certain modern "improvements" leave much to be desired. Many local inhabitants resented the so called advance of the town preferring to say "Let us bide as us be", but those of us who work in the town owe much to the foresight and investment of our forefathers who turned a small fishing village into a thriving seaside resort.

This panoramic view of Paignton in 1871 was taken from Keysfield Road. In the foreground are the houses of Belle Vue Road. From left to right, in the middle distance it is possible to identify the Congregational (now United Reformed) Church; The Gerston's railway engine house, now the booking hall; Gerston Hotel; Nell Pope's Hotel; Garfield (or Town Bank) Terrace, above which appears houses at the junction of Torquay and Polsham Roads; and the Singer's "Wigwam" beyond that. Victoria Street is the white line between the Gerstons and the Gerston Hotel!

Another panoramic view, taken from Primley Park looking SE, shows the terrace to the left of centre in Eastern Side of Conway Road. Immediately above is Tower House being built by Mr Bailey—ultimately the Marist Convent. Above that appears the first St Andrews Church in Dartmouth Road adjacent to the railway bridge in Roundham Road. The few houses middle right are at the bottom of St Michael's Road with Romlyn in the background with Goodrington beyond.

This photograph was taken of Goodrington North Sands looking towards Roundham Head during the late nineteenth century. The path on the left known as Breakneck Hill still exists, and the promenade as we know it today was constructed between 1929 and 1934. The PUDC took advantage of the generous grants made by central government for unemployment relief works, and 'The Prom' was officially opened in May 1936 by Sir Robert Horne, chairman of the GWR which has contributed so much to Paignton's growth. The total cost of building the retaining sea wall and terraced footpaths was £21,312.2s.0d. Combined with these works were the filling in of May's Pool and laying out of Goodrington Park and boating lakes, providing an immense and unsuspected source of revenue during the next 50 years.

Broadsands is an outlying suburb a few miles to the south of Paignton and this picture shows how it was in the early 1900s before any development took place. Blue Waters estate currently stands on the left hand hill, whilst Broadsands Avenue fills the rough ground in the centre. Building started in the early 1930s, was stopped during World War II, and resumed in the 1950s. Blue Waters Estate is built on land at one time part of Lord Churston's Estate. The viaduct, one of two constructed by the Torbay and Dartmouth Railway in 1860, the South Devon Railway assuming responsibility two years later, is still in use today requiring minimal maintenance. Beyond is Broadsands Beach and Elberry Lane where the Elberry Estate has since been built.

The Paignton Cottage Hospital was built by the Singer brothers, Adam, Mortimer and Washington, and was opened on 17 February 1891. The total cost including land and building etc was £2,885.5s.9d. The hospital was supported purely by voluntary contributions up to its absorption in to the National Health Service in 1948. Still part of the life of Paignton, only the entrance porch remains of the original building.

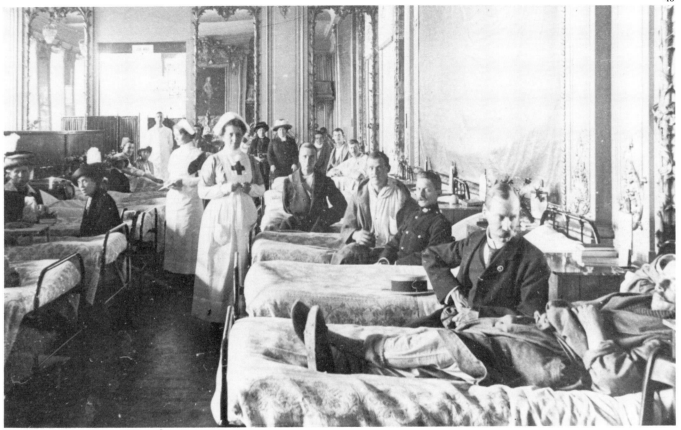

At the outbreak of World War I, Paris Singer loaned his Oldway Mansion to be used as a hospital for the expected wounded servicemen some of whom can be seen here recuperating in the ballroom. It became known as The American Women's War Hospital because it was supported by generous contributions from the United States. It was visited by Queen Mary, wife of George V in November 1914. Thousands of men from all regiments, ships and countries, were nursed back to health by a tremendous team of doctors and nurses, many men then returning to the battlefields to pay the supreme sacrifice with their lives.

This is Isaac Singer's "Wigwam", looking eastward from Little Oldway. It was designed by George Souden Bridgman, was completed in 1875 a year after Isaac's death and inherited by his son Paris. The tremendous conservatory was 70 feet wide and 60 feet tall, and occupied the site of the present car park. The sloping drive in front of the conservatory leads up to the main entrance at that time on the first floor.

In 1904 Paris Singer, enamoured with French architecture, had Oldway completely remodelled. Pillars were set up on the north and east facades, a mansard-roof was added, a magnificent pink marble staircase was installed, and the entrance was lowered to its present ground floor level. At one time Oldway provided a home for Isadora Duncan whose assignation with Paris caused no small scandal at the time. When Paris died in June 1932 he willed that when the Torbay Country Club relinquished its lease on the mansion it should be offered to the local authority. Requisitioned by the RAF for the whole of World War II, Oldway Mansion was purchased in 1945 by the Paignton Urban District Council for £45,000 and is now one of the finest municipal buildings in the country.

The Nest Holiday Camp, opened in 1925, was Paignton's first and this photograph was taken in the early 1930s from Kings Ash Hill. The road on the left is Foxhole Road, and centre rear is Colley End Road. The Waterleat Estate now occupies the field on the right and a sheltered housing association has built on the site of the camp.

Conway Road looking across Totnes Road towards Primley Park shows numerous villas but no bungalows or garages!

This is a very old photograph, taken in 1870, showing Church Street from outside the Parish Church looking towards Hyde Road Corner. The large building behind the wall was the vicarage and the railings are still there.

A later photograph taken from the same spot—the wall on the right of the picture can be seen in both. Starkey Knight and Ford, the local brewers, owned the property to the west of the old Vicarage, at the time of this photo (1970s) taken over by Whitbreads. Some of their buildings have since been demolished and some integrated within a sheltered housing project (called St John's Court) which has received an architectural award for its design.

The demolition of Croft Hotel, Hyde Road in 1963, made way for the Crossways Shopping Centre.

Old Paigntonians will no doubt remember the original Torbay Mills retail shop in Winner Street, almost opposite the Globe Inn. This photograph was taken about 1935 and clearly shows adverts for the three Paignton Cinemas: The Picture House, now Torbay Cinema, the Regent in Station Square and The Electric Palace ("The Bug House") in Totnes Road.

These ladies are all hard at work at the Paignton Sanitary Laundry in Totnes Road. Note the gas fired hand irons.

For deliveries the Paignton Sanitary Laundry had this van, photographed possibly in Torquay Road near the Gerston Hall. The laundry was situated on the Totnes Road, just above Collingwood Road, and the hooter (7.50 am and 5.00 pm) was a familiar local time signal and fire alarm until the outbreak of the Second World War.

The workers shown here are from Battershall & Sons Coach Works in St Michael's Road on the corner of Batson Gardens, probably around 1900.

The men of the Paignton Fire Brigade can be seen here with their new 1920 Leyland Fire Engine and escape ladder, outside the old fire station between New Street and Palace Avenue. The Leyland engine, their pride and joy, replaced the old horse drawn vehicle. The solid tyres were replaced by pneumatic ones in 1930. In 1911 the brass helmets were purchased for the sum of 16/3d each. With the opening of the new fire station in Cecil Road in 1973 the old premises were acquired by the Torbay Borough Council and used for the manufacture and storage of Ice Cream.

This photograph shows Mr Alan and Mrs Coleman outside Paignton Co-op, butcher's and fishmonger's shop in Winner Street, Christmas 1918. They sold a complete range of Christmas fare from tangerines to Christmas trees. The young man on the left is Mr S. J. Wills of Paignton.

The delivery van was for Andrews' Stores, for many years situated on the corner of Garfield Road. The building burnt down in the mid 1980s and has been rebuilt. The photograph was taken outside the railway station goods entrance.

The staff of Dellers Cafe took time off from their merrymaking to pose for this photograph during their annual party around 1949. Also pictured in the main ballroom is Mr Craze, the manager and one time Chairman of the PUDC, shown in the centre of the group.

Here we have the Paignton Amateur Athletic Club in about 1930. Seated in the centre is Syd Cooksley, on his left are Harold Pearson and Arthur Toms. Raymond Hole, Jack French, Charlie and Millie Gilbert, Jack Waters, Harry Mumford and Bill Bridgman are among the members.

Maidenway Road Air Raid Wardens are pictured here at the junction of Lammas Lane. The cabins behind the barbed wire fence were placed there from Goodrington to provide shelter for the Home Guard unit keeping an eye on the reservoir behind the wall.

This photograph of the Paignton Urban District Council in 1909 includes Mr Lambshead who was the founder of Dellers Stores, originally in Winner Street in the 1860s, then Palace Avenue from 1890. He also built Queens Park Mansions early this century. Fred Sarson founded the well known chemists, Sarson & Son at Maypole Corner. W. Drew was a member of the local building firm family. Mr Westlake was a councillor and chairman of the water committee responsible for the building of Paignton's first water supply from Venford on Dartmoor.
Front row (l to r): W. Drew, J. R. Mill (Clerk), E. Foxworthy
middle row: Fred Sarson (Vice Chairman), H. A. Parnell, J P (Chairman), W. J. Ham
back row: Dr H. N. Collier, J. S. Huggins, W. Lambshead, B. P. Milsom, E. Westlake, R. Moore, R. Coombes

The last gathering of Paignton Urban District Council on 30 September 1967 photographed at Oldway Mansion.

Front row (l to r): G. K. Foster, Mrs Fraser-James, Jimmy Tremeer, Frank Martin, Ken Walker, Jack Kingsland, Wally Beasley, Mrs Heath, Mrs Walton, Mrs Basildon, John Cole.
middle row: John Hayman, Bill Preston, Syd Elliott, Quentin Buckland, -, John Ellswood, Bill Chidgey, Leon Jones, Jack Bennett.
back row: Fred Bidgood, Ray Snell, -, Frank Charlesworth, Arthur Agar, John Bewley, Graham Lorraine.